# SWING TIPS YOU SHOULD FORGET

## BY MICHAEL JACOBS & SHAUN WEBB

### WITH MATTHEW RUDY

Printed in the United States of America

First Printing, 2014

ISBN-13: 978-1505208467
ISBN-10: 1505208467

X Golf U LLC
105 Clancy Road
Manorville, NY  11949
www.xgolfschool.com

*Designed by Tim Oliver (timothypoliver.com)*

*For students of the golf swing,*
*past and present.*

# CONTENTS

### FOREWORD BY DAVID TOMS / 9

# FOREWORD

BY DAVID TOMS

'm not an old guy, but I guess I'm old enough to be considered old school. I've always considered myself a guy who plays by feel. It wasn't until I was almost out of college at LSU that I ever saw my swing on video, and until a few years ago, I had never been on any kind of launch monitor.

But since I've gotten to know Shaun Webb and Michael Jacobs, I've been introduced to a new world in golf instruction. The knowledge and technological expertise they have has not only been a big help to my game, but also a key part of the new golf academy I started in Shreveport as a part of my David Toms

Foundation. I'm fortunate to have Shaun as my instructor and the director of the academy, and he's helping me build a facility that helps kids take the next step in this game—whether that means improving from beginner status or growing into a college scholarship player.

Taking that next step is something we all want to do as players. I've heard every golf tip you can imagine in more than 25 years as a tour player, and I've probably tried them all. What makes the information in this book great—and the technology that supports it—is that it removes so much of the guesswork. Knowing you're working on the right things—whether that's improving your arm speed or adjusting your head position, two things you're going to read about shortly—is so crucial, both in terms of saving time and building confidence.

I know that when Shaun works with me on my swing using the GEARS system we have here at my golf academy, I can get a real "fingerprint" of what I'm doing when I'm really hitting the ball well. And when I start to struggle, I can get back on the machine and see what I'm doing differently. I get real, immediate feedback after every swing, and I know exactly what I need to do to make an improvement. I'm getting information that helps me get my swing to where I can hit the different shots I need out on the course, and ultimately to make a score—which is what my job is all about.

The information isn't a guess, and it isn't a generic tip that's been taken for granted and recycled over the years.

In *Swing Tips You Should Forget*, Mike and Shaun will use cutting-edge research and technology to actually simplify how you approach your own game. Instead of trying to focus on dozens of different tips that may or may not apply to you—and might even be obsolete—you're getting a clear guide to making an efficient, modern swing. This kind of teaching is the future of our game—both on the Tour and for the regular player.

And you don't need a GEARS system or TrackMan to take advantage of it.

Enjoy the book, and come out to see Shaun and me at the David Toms Academy in Shreveport, Louisiana, or visit Mike's X Golf School at Rock Hill Country Club on Long Island, in New York.

**DAVID TOMS**
**PGA Tour player and 2001 PGA Champion**
**Shreveport, LA.,**
**October 8, 2014**

# INTRODUCTION

I n the 120 or so years the game has been professionally taught, teachers have accumulated and shared a huge amount of information about what the body and club do (or should do) during the swing. During that same time, millions of players at every skill level have been on the lookout for the lesson, tip, drill or secret move that would help them hit better shots.

Out of all that effort and searching, some of the most popular (or oldest) ideas have been talked about so much that they've been accepted as the "truth." If you walked down the line at a driving range in 1950, you probably heard a guy telling one of his friends he missed that last shot because he didn't keep his head down. Almost 65 years later, you'll hear somebody say the same thing after a topped shot. "I picked my head up."

You can't turn ten pages in a golf magazine without reading about the ideal swing plane, or how average players need to stop flipping their wrists at the ball and start retaining more lag in the downswing to produce power like the tour players do.

In *Swing Tips You Should Forget*, we're going to examine eight of these "classic" pieces of golf instruction and explain why following that advice will actually hurt your game the way it's played today, not help it. They're ideas you've certainly heard dozens of times each–but probably don't realize are incomplete, outdated or just plain wrong. Besides keeping your head down, creating more lag and stopping the wrist flip through impact, we're also going to cover pausing at the top, keeping your arms out of the swing, making the same swing for every club, swinging on plane and swinging the club down the target line–a collection of tips that are to this day keeping tens of thousands of players busy at the range.

At the end of the book, we'll share two of the instruction ideas we think will be an important part of the new generation of biomechanically sound teaching.

Our goal isn't to be contrary or controversial. And the lessons and drills you'll learn in each of the chapters aren't guesswork. Our teaching is based on the latest biomechanical and golf instruction research, and backed up with images and data from the most cutting edge measuring and diagnostic equipment in the world of golf.

The images you'll see throughout the book come from the GEARS system–the Golf Evaluation and Research System, which is a combination of powerful software, eight high-speed cameras and motion-capture suit fitted with 26 markers. The system tracks the body and club and analyzes the data from more than 600 images per swing, and is accurate within 0.2 millimeters. Used in conjunction with force plates on the ground, we can get an extremely accurate picture of what any player does with his swing—and compare it to any other golfer.

We know what you're doing, and we know what the best players in the world are doing. With all the new and accurate data available, we can tell which techniques and tips are useful, and which ones are counterproductive.

Get ready to change how you think about golf instruction.

Before we start, here's a little more information about us.

**MICHAEL JACOBS**

My teaching studio at Rock Hill Country Club in Manorville, Long Island might be the most technologically advanced on the East Coast, with 3D imaging, force plates and a battery of high-definition cameras.

But it all started with a persimmon wood and a Flying Lady golf ball, on par-3 course in Commack, Long Island, with my dad.

I hit that first shot over the green on an 80-yard par-3 at age six, and I was hooked. I started using the family VCR to record the weekly PGA Tour events, and played back the swings in slow motion so I could see what made players like Payne Stewart look so good.

I begged my parents for real clubs and lessons, and by the time I was a teenager, I was competing in some regional junior events. Every summer, the days I wasn't playing in a tournament went exactly the same way. My mom dropped me off at Smithtown Landing at eight in the morning, and I'd play 18 holes, then spend an hour on short game, two hours on putting and another hour on full shots at the range.

As I moved into junior golf, I started taking lessons from one of the most decorated teachers in the U.S. But even after investing thousands of hours in the game and thousands of my parents' dollars in lessons, I saw my game not only level off but become more inconsistent.

When I got to Methodist University in Fayetteville, NC, I decided to take the PGA's playing ability test to start the process of becoming a teaching professional. After an even-par first round, I completely fell apart the next day. I had to make a six-footer on the last hole to shoot 84 and qualify on the number. I shook that putt in, and immediately decided my future wasn't as a player.

Walking off the last green, I decided I was going to commit my life to figuring out a better way for people to play golf. I checked out every book on physics and biomechanics in the Methodist library, and tracked down every golf instruction book I could find. I'd even prop the golf books behind my textbooks in other classes so I could study as much as possible.

I was fortunate enough to get a job at Rock Hill when I was 21, and by 1999, I opened the X Golf School there. Fifteen years and 20,000 students later, my school is thriving and I'm proud to have been recognized by my peers as the Metropolitan PGA Teacher of the Year.

Technology is a big part of my day-to-day as a teacher, but that doesn't mean I don't have an understanding or appreciation for what's come before. After I read everything the Methodist library had to offer, I started tracking down as many of the classic (and obscure) golf instruction books I could find. I've built a collection of nearly 700 volumes—everything from the first instruction book written by a golf professional, Willie Park Jr.'s *"The Game of Golf"* of 1895 to David Williams' *"The Science of the Golf Swing"* (which was and is still the best instruction book ever done).

Jim Barnes' book "A Picture Analysis of Golf Strokes" was the first one to use high-speed photography to show the golf swing, in 1919. Now, with the help of my friend Shaun Webb and plenty of spirited discussion from a group of like-minded teachers and biomechanical experts, I'm excited to be a part of something that hopefully helps change the way the golf swing is discussed. Why use "folklore," as my friend Brian Manzella calls some of the old ideas, when you can use hard data?

**SHAUN WEBB**

My introduction to the game came in a way very similar to Michael's. I was five years old when my dad started taking me and my brother Cory to Island Country Club in my hometown of Deer Isle, Maine. I had a few cut down clubs, and my dad—a scratch player—showed me enough of the basics to get me started.

It wasn't long before I was playing all day, every day in the short window when it wasn't snowing (and sometimes when it was). I moved up the ranks as a player in junior golf, but my first love was always learning about swing technique.

I don't know if I got more enjoyment out of trying the tips-from the latest golf magazine myself or interpreting them for my friends as a "teacher," but the teaching inclination only got stronger when my parents got a video camera. I'm sure they planned on shooting home movies, but I took the camera and set it up in the backyard everyday. I recorded thousands of my swings, and compared them in slow motion to VCR recordings of tour player swings I made from the tournament coverage.

After a successful junior career, I went to college in Florida to continue competing. A series of back issues kept me from playing as much as I wanted, so I turned my focus to learning as much as I could about the swing. As my back started to heal, I made my way around Orlando and took lessons from some of the greatest teachers in the world—with the hope that I could both learn more about the golf swing in general and improve my swing in a way that would put less pressure on my back.

But after over a year of lessons, my ball-striking actually got worse. I was trying to eliminate a hook, but the advice I got— swing more to the right—made it worse. I think I've actually received first-hand seven of the eight bad swing lessons we talk about in this book, from some of the most famous teachers in the business.

At my lowest point as a player, I knew that I needed to find a way to help golfers out of the trap I had gotten myself into. I've been down most of the wrong roads, and it's my job to try to help players avoid the time and energy it takes to U-turn their way out of them.

As a teacher, I've dedicated the last 14 years to improving my knowledge base and coaching skills. I'm lucky to be able to work with and coach one my of golfing heroes, David Toms, at his academy here in Shreveport. The first I ever saw of Michael

Jacobs was on one of his terrific instruction videos he posted on YouTube. Soon after, I happened to see him walking the floor at the PGA Merchandise Show in Orlando, and I introduced myself.

We got to be great friends, and in the years since, we've had hundreds of hours of conversation about the subjects you're going to read about shortly. It's been exciting to see it come together on paper (or the screen of an e-book!), and very satisfying to know that golfers of all levels will have a blueprint for incorporating new, better information into their game.

# NOTES

# 1

## MAKE THE
## SAME SWING FOR
## EVERY CLUB

I f you're older than about 35, you can probably remember
first-hand when golf equipment looked a lot different than
it does today. The huge 450-cc drivers in bags today are
obviously different than their counterparts from the 1940s or
1950s, but irons have changed dramatically, too. When the average 15-handicapper in 1950 had a shot with a 4-iron, he or she
looked down at a tiny butter knife of a blade, compared to the
forgiving perimeter-weighted iron—or hybrid—of today.

Considering how hard it was to consistently hit the middle of
those tiny clubheads—and what the result was if you missed—it

**Modern drivers (left) are 460 cc, with a center of gravity higher and farther away from the shaft than a 200 cc persimmon club from the 1970s.**

isn't hard to understand why generations of teachers tried to simplify the swing as much as possible for average players. They promoted the idea of a consistent swing you used for every shot—starting with a little chip shot and growing up to a full swing with irons and on through to the driver using the same geometry for all swings.

Back in the day, that persimmon driver wasn't so different than the rest of the clubs in the bag. The center of gravity wasn't very far back from the shaft, and the tiny head didn't really promote the idea that you should swing up on the ball off the tee to launch it.

You can probably see the problem.

If you use your same wedge or 7-iron swing—which makes

contact with the ball as the club is descending—with your driver, you're going to struggle to hit consistent shots, and you won't get nearly the distance you should.

In the most basic terms, you will release the club later and make a descending blow with your irons. With the lighter, longer, bigger driver, you need to start releasing the club sooner so you have time to get the head square and launch the ball. If you really struggle with your driver, but hit your iron shots great (or vice versa), it's probably happening because you're using the same kind of swing for both flavors of shot.

There's no reason to get discouraged and think that golf is hard enough without having to learn two different swings. The nuts and bolts of what you need to do are the same. You'll just need to make some adjustments. It's no different than what they do with the Iron Byron hitting machines. When they switch clubs, there are some tweaks they make to how the machine releases the club so that it doesn't leave the face open and slice a driver or close the face too early and hook an iron.

Let's pause for a second and talk about what "releasing" the club is for the purposes of this discussion, so we're all on the same page. Your hands move on a curved path up and around on the backswing, and then down and around on the downswing into the through-swing.

At a point in the downswing, you have to unload the club so that it moves outside the hand path and moves toward the ball— so that it eventually lines up with the left hand. This "release torque"—the actual snap of the club with the wrists in the direction the club is travelling—is the release.

As you work your way through the bag from wedge to driver, you're going to calibrate the point in your downswing when you

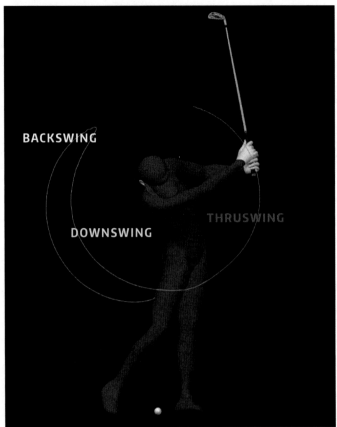

BACKSWING

DOWNSWING

THRUSWING

The white part of the curve is the path the hands take back. The yellow indicates the path the hands take down to the ball, while the orange indicates the through swing.

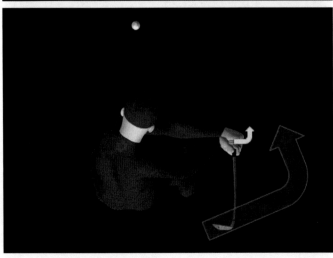

"Wrist torque" is the snap of the wrists in the direction the club is traveling.

The downswing lasts only about a quarter of a second. For the release to happen at the right time in the swing, you have to apply torque to the club much earlier than expected.

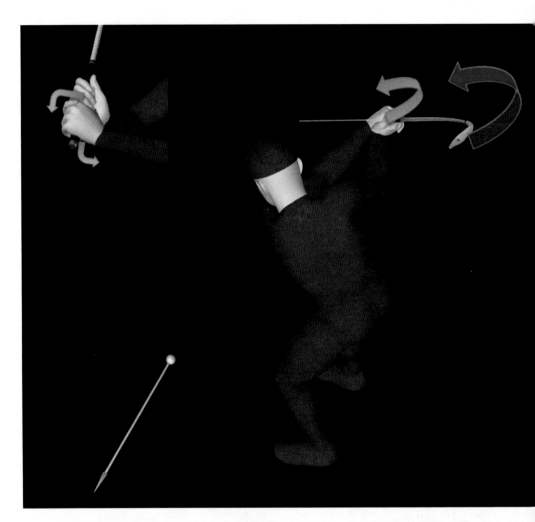

The release "feel" is that you're pushing with the right hand in the direction of your right pinkie finger while simultaneously pulling with the left hand in the direction of the left pinkie. This push-pull activates a good portion of your club-head speed. Without it, you're costing yourself distance and consistent contact.

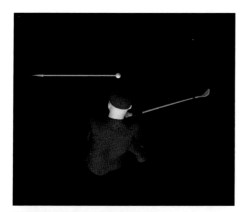

WEDGE RELEASE POINT

These three images show the different timing of when the release starts. It happens later in the downswing with shorter clubs. The top image is a wedge, the middle is an iron and the bottom is a driver.

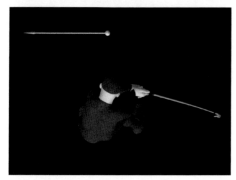

IRON RELEASE POINT

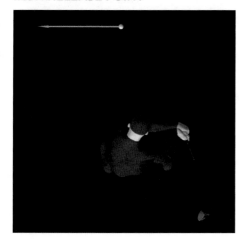

DRIVER RELEASE POINT

need to initiate that release torque. It isn't complicated, but it will take some practice and attention.

With the short irons, the club doesn't have as much distance to travel, and the release can happen later in the downswing and still have enough time to get the club in line at impact. As the clubs get longer, though, you'll need to start the release torque earlier in the downswing. Think of it as a highway exit ramp, and your short irons are sports cars while the longer clubs are tractor trailers. With the sports car, you can get away with more speed and steering later in the turn. In a tractor trailer, you need to start turn-

**27**

ing earlier and accelerate in a gradual, controlled way.

For example, with the driver, you're going to want to feel that by the time your hands get down to your back leg the clubhead is tickling the grass. It won't really, but it's a great way to imprint the sensation of unloading clubhead sooner. From that point, you aren't just dragging the clubhead (figuratively) along the grass through impact. You're matching that move with a second snap of the wrists in the new direction the club is travelling—which is towards impact. This flexion and extension of the wrists—which we will talk about in Chapter 6—harnesses that last bit of acceleration to the clubhead and helps the forearms square the face at impact.

As you work your way through the bag, you'll probably find that the shortest and longest clubs are the easiest to fit into this framework. Short irons give you the most time and room for error. Once you adjust your stance and setup to suit a ball that's up on a tee—by playing the ball farther forward, which puts the center of your body behind the ball and promotes an upward strike—the earlier release torque is going to provide you with better launch.

It gets slightly trickier with longer clubs like fairway woods—and, to a lesser degree, hybrids. The ball is still on the ground for those shots, but you need to start the release earlier to be able to get the longer shaft and lighter head out, around and into line by the time you get to impact. With these clubs, you're trying to make your strike as level as possible. For example, if you're striking downward four degrees with your 7-iron, a downward angle of about two degrees would be ideal for a hybrid.

One piece of this puzzle that almost always gets overlooked is how your release point—and how much you hit up or down on

**You can clearly see the difference in body angles between these two setup positions. These are from Ryder Cup hero Ian Poulter. The left is his driver, and right is a middle iron.**

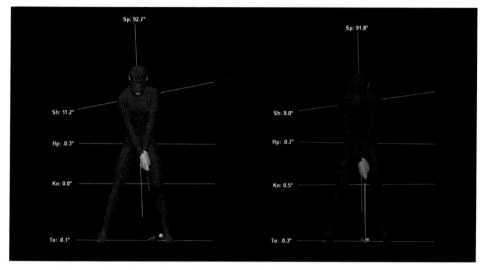

**Adjusting the set up to promote an upward blow with a driver and a downward blow with irons is instrumental for consistency throughout the entire bag.**

the shot—affects your aim. Systems like GEARS and TrackMan measure the angle of attack for the clubhead into the ball. For every degree your club is descending through impact, the path is being skewed inside-out, or out to the right. And for every degree the club is ascending, the path is being skewed outside-in, or to the left.

When you look at the bottom of Rickie Fowler's swing arc in GEARS, you can see how the position of the club in the arc is related to how the path changes.

Let's use a basic visual reference to reinforce that point. If you were to make a mark on a hula hoop to signify where the ball would be and hold the hoop at the same angle as your swing, you could see a visual representation of where your clubhead is traveling throughout the swing. If you move to a point earlier on the hoop–farther away from the target–the clubhead would be heading more toward the ground and more to the right of the target. Move to a point later in the hoop and the opposite is true–you would be traveling more into the air and to the left.

What does this mean in real life, on the course?

It means that when you're hitting a short iron, you're going to have to either change something in your swing or adjust your aim to the left to account for the difference in your swing path. The opposite is true with the driver. If all else is equal and neutral, an ascending blow will cause an outside-in path, so you'll have to adjust for it either with swing or aim.

Aim is a lot easier to change (and doesn't require any coordination!), and we've built a simple chart that helps you figure out how much adjustment you need to make based on the club you're hitting.

**AIM CHART**

| LENGTH OF SHOT | AIM AMOUNT BASED ON TARGET IN THE DISTANCE |
| --- | --- |
| 100 yards | 5 yards left |
| 150 yards | 6 yards left |
| 200 yards | 4 yards left |
| 250 yards | 12 yards right |
| 300 yards | 15 yards right |

Technical Notes on Aim Chart:
X Golf School Standard Attack Angles were used in Aim Calculations
PW 6 degrees down
7 Iron 4 degrees down
Hybrid 2 degrees down
Driver 3 degrees up
X Golf School Standard Vertical Swing Planes were used in Aim Calculations
PW 64 degrees
7 Iron 61 degrees
Hybrid 58 degrees
Driver 47 degrees

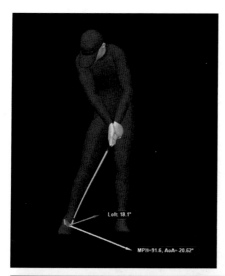

A downward movement of the clubhead through impact produces an inside-out path to the right of the target.

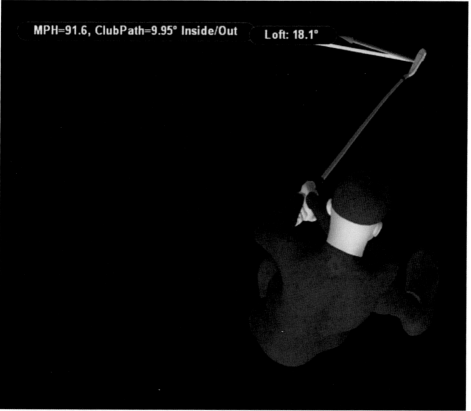

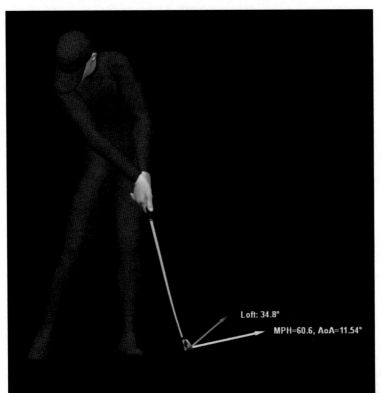

An upward movement of the clubhead through impact produces an outside-in path to the left of the target.

Loft: 34.8°

MPH=60.6, AoA=11.54°

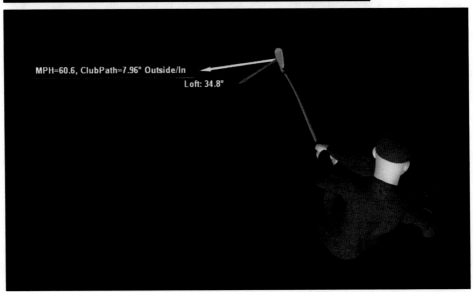

MPH=60.6, ClubPath=7.96° Outside/In

Loft: 34.8°

# NOTES

# 2

## LAG
## IT!

**F**ollowing any of the "classic" tips we will be talking about in this book is a recipe for disaster for your game. But of all of them, the idea of needing more lag is probably the one that has caused average players the worst problems over the last 20 years.

We're obviously big fans of technology in golf instruction. You're seeing it in the GEARS images throughout the book. But, ironically enough, this whole "lag problem" started ruining golf swings just about the time when teachers started getting wide access to video teaching systems.

Out of the box, systems like V-1 and JC Video have a noble goal. They work in concert with a video camera and laptop to give the teacher the chance to overlay a video of a student's swing with directional and reference lines and audio commentary to reinforce the instruction point he or she is trying to make.

Most of the systems also come with a library of tour player swings for the teacher to use as side-by-side comparisons. You can watch what you do and compare it to what Tiger Woods or Jack Nicklaus does.

There's nothing wrong with using good swings as references. We do it all the time with GEARS.

The problems start happening when you misinterpret what a player is actually doing with his swing. For 20 years, the conventional teaching on the subject of lag–defined as the angle between the lead forearm and the shaft on the downswing–has

been that tour players have a lot of it, so it must be good to try to get more of it.

You don't have to look any farther than Rickie Fowler or Sergio Garcia for proof of this obsession–and misunderstanding–of lag.

Rickie and Sergio are not big guys–Rickie is 5-foot

**Lag is defined as the angle between the lead forearm and the shaft of the club—measured from the outside, not the inside.**

**36**

**Rickie Fowler's lag angle increases from 100 degrees at the top of the backswing to 110 degrees when his arms are parallel to the ground on the downswing.**

9 and 150 pounds while Sergio is 5-foot-10 and 160 pounds. When Sergio turned pro in 1999, everybody had something to say about his swing, which features Ben Hogan-style lag and late release in the downswing. The same happened when Rickie started on tour in 2009. Teachers—and TV analysts—across the country freeze-framed Rickie's swing in the middle of the downswing and told students and viewers that the reason Rickie hits it so far as a little guy is because he holds a lot of lag until late and then snaps the clubhead into the ball.

"Holds" is the key word here.

If you look at 3D data of Rickie's swing in the late stages of his backswing and compare it to a point frozen in the downswing, when his left arm is parallel to the ground, you'll see the angle between that left forearm and the shaft has increased 10 degrees.

But Rickie—or any other tour player—isn't "producing" that increase in lag angle by physically manipulating his wrists and hands (applying a negative release torque, in technical terms) on the downswing. That lag angle is a natural result of great body sequencing and a hand path that conserves the outward movement of the club.

In other words, Rickie isn't forcing the club into that lagged position. The movements he creates with his body lead to a chain reaction, and that lagged position is a result of that chain reaction. You see it the most dramatically on smaller, more flexible players like Sergio and Rickie, who really produce a lot of quick body movements.

Why does this matter?

Because if you're trying to physically create more lag in your swing with your wrists to deal with a "casting" or early release problem, you're not fixing the problem. You're making it worse.

Unless you address the sequencing of your body, two things will happen. Either you'll hold that "extra" lag into the downswing and never unload the club or you won't square the face at impact and produce a glancing blow.

To produce solid shots, stop thinking about your lag angle and concentrate on the two main pieces that really do produce solid, long shots: body sequencing and hand path.

Let's take them one at a time.

Tour players swing the club very differently from each other, but one quality they share is great body sequencing. By the time the club is slowing down at the top of the backswing and getting ready to transition to moving back around toward the ball, the body has already started to move forward (both laterally and rotationally). The movement forward is initiated by a push and a twist from the right foot. We will get into this push and twist— what it is and how to do it—in more detail in Chapter 3.

When you initiate the sequence the right way, the body starts to move laterally, toward the target, and the arms naturally move closer in towards the body—which promotes that "lag angle" everyone wants. The feel you're looking for is one of turning your torso so that it pushes up against the bicep of your left or lead arm—which we'll talk more about in Chapter 5.

The second piece to the puzzle is hand path—another subject that hasn't always been well understood by teachers. Fortunately, with 3D technology—and a really smart guy like Dr. Steven Nesbit doing the research—we now know that the path the hands take from the top of the backswing down around through to the finish isn't circular.

In reality, every player's hands move down in a unique path

RICKIE FOWLER                    IAN POULTER

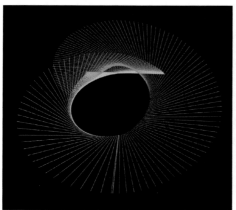 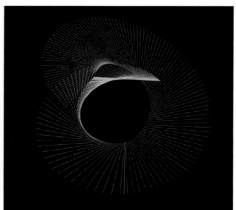

**A graphic representing the path a player's hands take is like the fingerprint of a golf swing.**

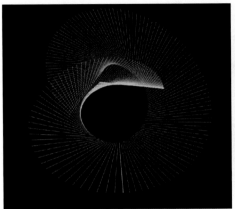 

GREG NORMAN                    DAVID TOMS

that looks more like a seashell. If you diagram that path—something GEARS does really well—you get what amounts to the fingerprint of a golf swing. By looking at this collection of diagrams, you can see some of the similarities between players who are known for hitting it long and/or straight. Rickie Fowler and Greg Norman have the same "egg-shaped" curve to their hand path starting at shoulder height in the downswing, which represents the clubhead changing direction and the hands taking the widest route possible around to the ball.

Players with a more circular path, like David Toms and Ian Poulter, don't create as much of that dynamic tension in their hand path. They're not "cracking the whip" as hard. Toms' hand path pattern is the most circular of any we've captured with 3D measurement—which makes him as close to an Iron Byron hitting machine as possible. He produces a smooth, continual release throughout the downswing, which doesn't create the most power, but has made him one of the most accurate ball-strikers of all time.

When the average player tries to "produce" lag, he usually gets to the top of the backswing and then pulls his hands straight toward the ball as hard as he can while trying to hold onto the

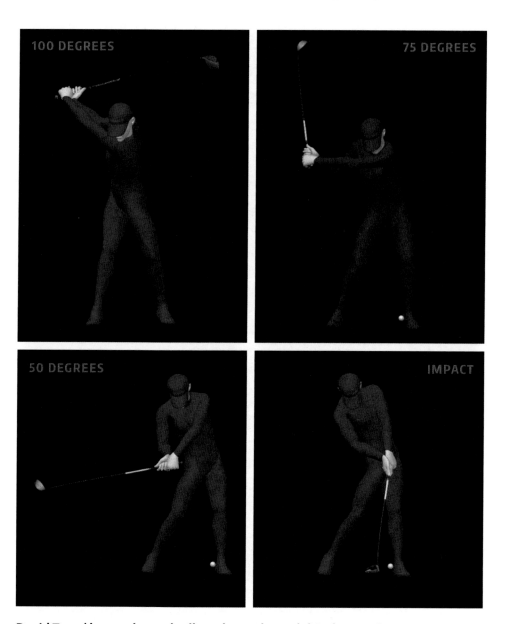

David Toms' lag angle gradually reduces through his downswing, from 100 degrees at the top to 75 degrees when the arms are parallel to the ground and 50 degrees when the club gets down to parallel to the ground. His focus is a smooth, orderly release.

A common average-player mistake is the driving of the hands straight down toward the ball from the top.

angle between the shaft and the forearms.

This is what it looks like when a 25-handicapper tries to do that in GEARS.

Yanking the hands down that way actually has the opposite effect to what the player intended—with the clubhead releasing even earlier and the lag angle reducing way too soon.

You can use a wall to give you a sense for how this sequencing should work. Go to the top of your backswing and position yourself so that the butt end of the club is three inches from the wall. Make some slow downswing transitions so that the end of the handle scrapes against the wall on the way down, which promotes the wider hand path you need.

It's a subtle but important point. The path your hands take—not any holding action with the wrists and hands—will cause the shaft to delay or lag. If you try to hold your wrists back to create lag, or pull your hands toward the ball, you're going to make the club move outward—or cast—even earlier.

With better body sequencing and an improved hand path, your club will naturally trail behind the arms on the downswing, and you'll get some of that "stored power" and "late hit" tour players famously have.

# NOTES

# 3

# PAUSE
# AT THE TOP

Terms and phrases like "rhythm," "getting too quick" and "hitting from the top" have become a basic part of the golf instruction language because a lot of players have some basic problems related to those ideas. They aren't coordinating their body motion back and through the ball.

But the basic piece of advice you usually hear as a first step toward fixing some of those problems–pausing at the top of the backswing–has its own set of problems.

It starts with a misunderstanding of what is really happening within the dynamic motion of a good swing.

If you look at video of any top player and focus just on the club, there's obviously a point where the club stops moving on its arc back away from the ball and starts the transition around and toward it again. The point where the club stops is generally considered to be the "top" of the backswing.

But just because the club has stopped at that point doesn't mean the rest of the body isn't in a state of motion. In fact, good players have already started moving their hips and then their upper bodies into the downswing before the club reaches the top. It's actually the tension between the unwinding of the body and the continued winding of the arms and club that stores a lot of energy to be used down at the ball.

In reality, if you do slow everything down to a stop at the top, you're robbing yourself of the body speed and tension that produces distance—and you're not doing anything to address those rhythm or "too quick transition" issues.

What is really causing those problems?

Usually it's a case of accelerating a segment of the body in the wrong amount at the wrong time. One of the most common examples comes from the desire to increase shoulder turn as much as possible to increase power. This translates into a lot of late, fast upper body speed at a time when the upper body should be slowing its winding phase and getting ready to un-wind. This promotes an equally big and fast unwinding of the upper body too soon in the downswing—before the lower body starts to move toward the target—and you see that big lurch for-ward and down with the head as the arms and club lose tension.

The swing happens fast, and it can be hard to feel exactly what's going on at a given time. But with a simple drill, you can signifi-cantly improve that chain reaction at the top of the backswing.

The curved arrows represent the direction you're trying to twist on the ground to make your hips turn toward the target. The orange arrow represents the force you're pushing on the right foot—as it would be shown on a force plate analysis device.

Suspend reality for a second and imagine that you're standing on a sheet of ice. Without using a ball, get in your normal stance. Now, make a slow backswing, and as your upper body gets close to the end of its turn away from the ball, feel it slow down even more while at the same time push with your right (trailing) foot as though you're trying to spin it away from the target. With your foot flat on the ground and spikes on, it won't actually spin out, but the pressure you're creating will trigger your hips to translate and turn the opposite direction—toward the target.

Responding to that trigger, the hips move and the upper body follows, which puts the arms and club in great, consistent position to come through last and fastest. Another creative way to think about the pushing movement of the right foot is to equate it to the accelerator on your car. You make the pushing motion and the car responds—but not instantly. You feel the push, a beat of time, and then the power comes from the motor. In this case, the motor is the unwinding of your hips.

If you can get the hips moving toward the target while the upper body is just finishing up the backswing, you're automatically in good shape to avoid the upper-body-first move that created the trouble in the first place.

As you practice this drill at faster and faster speeds, working up to your normal swing, one thing to remember is that sequencing is different than tempo. When you watch a player with a slow tempo and what looks like a dramatic pause at the top—like, say, Ernie Els—he's not really pausing his upper or lower body as much as he's making a more gradual transition from turning away to turning through.

Els is doing the exact same kinds of things in terms of body sequencing that somebody with a fast tempo—like Rickie Fowler—is doing. Neither of those guys is getting to the top of his swing and shutting down the movement of his body—even if that's something you hear them (or their instructor) say.

When a tour player does talk about consciously pausing at the top, it's more an example of a coming up with a feel or swing thought that produces the desired effect in the swing—even if the feel or thought doesn't match with what is really happening mechanically.

# NOTES

# 4

## SWING ON PLANE

N othing inspires a lot of energetic line drawing, confused looks from students—and arguments from teachers—like the subject of swing plane.

It's easy to understand why the subject gets so much attention. Thinking of the "ideal" swing as moving back and forth along a consistent line clicked out on a computer screen produces a straightforward goal for a student to try to reach.

But that idea has two major problems. First, "plane" is identified and measured a dozen different ways, and it's interpreted in a bunch of other ways by teachers and students. When you're

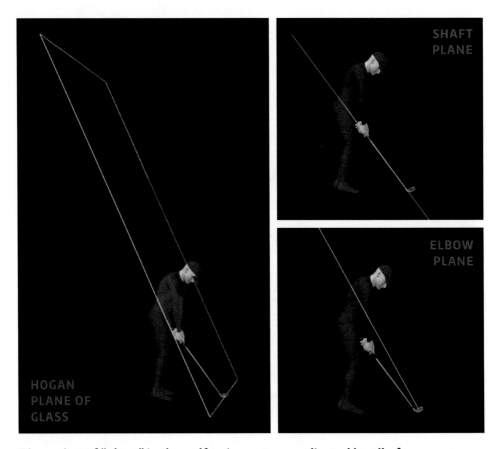

**Discussion of "plane" in the golf swing gets complicated by all of the different definitions and points of measure. We use the plane established by the clubhead as it moves throughout the swing.**

talking about plane, are you talking about Ben Hogan's plane of glass, angled to the ground and sitting on top of the shoulders?

Is it the shaft plane? Elbow plane? Jim Hardy's one-plane or two-plane swings? It's really hard to hit a target when you aren't sure what it is.

Assuming you can come up with a consensus on how "plane" should be defined—and we'll get to that in a minute—trying to make the club move on one dedicated plane throughout the

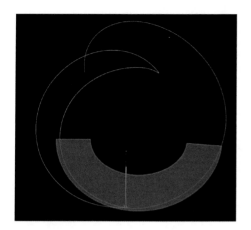

The only area of swing plane that really matters is the part shaded in blue—the execution phase (above). As you can see below, when the club goes up and around in the swing, it moves on a variety of planes.

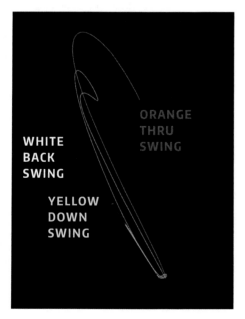

WHITE
BACK
SWING

ORANGE
THRU
SWING

YELLOW
DOWN
SWING

swing (or even two) is extremely difficult to do—and won't produce the best results.

What we're going to do here is establish a basic definition of what we think "plane" is, and show you where swinging "on plane" matters and where it doesn't.

The plane angle that matters is the one traced by where the center of the clubhead moves throughout the swing. The clubhead moves at various speeds throughout the swing—slowly during the takeaway and transition, and very fast near impact, for example. It's only during the part of the swing where the clubhead is moving very fast—during what we call the "execution phase," near the bottom of the swing arc around the ball—that you can expect to see a stabilized swing plane. This area is the part where you can focus most of your swing plane study.

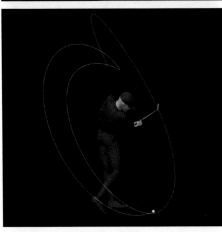

Where should you begin? Start thinking of your "plane" as a series of connected curves.

You have the curve represented by the movement of the clubhead back from the ball in the backswing (white).

You have the transition phase where the body shifts toward the target and the clubhead changes directions and the downswing (yellow) begins. After impact you have the through-swing curve (orange). The angle that these curves are on relative to the ground is your 'Swing Plane' at that moment in time.

How those curves work together determines your overall swing plane. As you can see in these images the plane

**The plane the club head makes at the bottom of the swing is the only area of the swing where the club has enough speed to stay on a stabilized swing plane.**

changes depending on where you are in your swing.

There's no specific plane angle you need to swing on– just broad parameters based on your body type and swing style. Your swing might be flatter or more upright. The pieces that matter are how consistently you transition the club from the backswing to the downswing and the repeatability of the motion of the clubhead during that 'execution phase.'

A great way to make this abstract concept more concrete in your own swing is to think about that zone where the club moves from shoulder down and around to the other shoulder specifically in terms of where the club is in relation to the ground.

**Mini-swings are a great way to train the shape of a stabilized swing plane.**

Unfortunately, understanding "real" swing plane where your swing fits isn't the end of the battle. You'll have to remember to filter what you hear about swing plane in, say, an instruction article in Golf Digest or a segment on Golf Channel. If the teacher you're watching or reading doesn't define plane in the same way, you could be applying some of the wrong solutions to your swing issues.

# NOTES

# 5

# KEEP THE ARMS OUT OF THE SWING

t's not any big revelation to point out that the game of today isn't played the same way as it was in 1900.

You don't even have to go back that far.

Just pull out the driver in your bag and compare it to the one Jack Nicklaus used in the 1960s, or even Greg Norman's from the 1990s.

We're not wearing tweed coats and ties when we play anymore, and we're using drivers with graphite shafts and heads three times the size of the average persimmon club. Watch film of Bobby Jones hitting shots in the 1920s and Rory McIlroy doing the same now and it's almost like watching two different sports.

Unfortunately, the whole thread of "keep your arms passive" in golf instruction comes from that Bobby Jones era—when it was more important to keep the whippy hickory shafts under control than to hit the ball a long way.

Today, golf courses are bigger, clubs are built more upright, and there's more demand for higher, longer shots. The game requires a different kind of swing—especially with a driver.

And it definitely requires a swing with more speed.

If you decided to play golf and keep the arms completely passive, you will never generate your maximum amount of clubhead speed. A study by a well-respected golf biomechanist showed that 23 percent of a good player's clubhead speed comes from the arms alone. That's a lot of yardage to give up if you're not interested in using that lever. In the most simple terms, the fastest way to get more clubhead speed is to activate your arms in the right way while recruiting the rest of your body to provide energy to help.

There's no question that a lot of the classic instruction directing the arms to stay passive—and the stacks of training aids that actively restrict arms—are trying to help the player who uses the arms in the wrong way or at the wrong time. You've probably even seen tour players make swings with a head cover under their lead arm in an effort to "stay connected."

We can debate whether or not that's something a tour player should be doing—the short answer is that it depends on the particular thing they're trying to do with their swing—but most tour players aren't dealing with a lack of clubhead speed. They also support the arm and upper body motion with good lower body action, and they use the ground effectively.

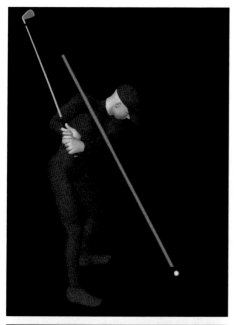

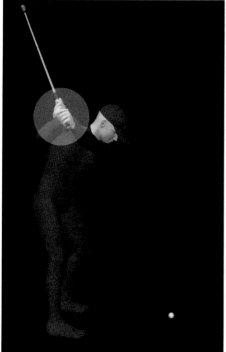

If the average player takes the "passive arms" advice to heart and tries to apply it, a few common things tend to happen. First, the arm plane on the backswing usually gets very flat.

When the arms move on this flat plane and stay below the back shoulder, you're set up to crash the club into the ground even if you make a strong, positive lower body motion. The natural compensation for this is to lift up your chest too much and too early to compensate, or to throw the club over the top to get to the ball.

Instead of improving the timing and consistency of the swing, making the arms pas-

**In a flat arm swing, the left hand never gets above the right shoulder (top). To gain more leverage, the arms need to move higher across the chest (bottom) and the left hand needs to at least reach the point of the right shoulder.**

sive has added more problems while also subtracting speed!

Your goal should be to incorporate the right amount of arm swing at the right time in your overall swing. In general terms, this means being able to see your left hand covering the point of your right shoulder if you turn your head slightly and look back.

That's a position virtually every golfer can get to—at minimum—even if you aren't tremendously flexible.

By getting your arms to raise in the backswing this way, you're actually engaging that critical lever in the swing that provides the final boost to clubhead speed. There's a reason why, when you're watching a PGA Tour event on television, that the commentators refer to a high, soft pitch as a "dead-arm shot." It's because the player has intentionally shut down that last speed lever to produce a controlled short-distance shot.

You'll get no argument here that shot can be useful from 50 yards, but if you're losing 10 or 15 miles per hour from your swing speed on a driver or a hybrid, you're going to struggle to get those shots up in the air consistently.

The downswing brings another huge problem many players run into—the classic "over-the-top" move. When you start your downswing by throwing the clubhead out away from your body and over the target line, so that it approaches the ball from the outside of the target line, you're coming over the top. It happens for a variety of reasons related to the sequencing of your swing and transfer of weight.

By improving the way you use your arms in the swing, you can eliminate the power-stealing over-the-top move for good. As we talked about in Chapter 3, the downswing happens as a chain reaction started at ground level. Your lower body and pelvis start shifting toward the target well ahead of the club. As you

**The clubhead moves into a flatter
position automatically as a result of good
body motion during the downswing.**

start turning your hips in the direction of the target, your torso
starts to follow.

Here's where the key "tour" move comes in. Get it right and
you'll transform your downswing—and your ballstriking and
power—almost overnight.

As your torso starts to turn toward the target, feel as though
you're creating pressure between the side of your chest and the
bicep of your lead arm. That little shot of pressure will cause the
lead arm to lower across your chest slightly, and the club will

move on a flatter trajectory—putting it in position to come into the ball on the correct downswing path. It's important to note that this flattening happens as a dynamic part of your transition—not because you're actively shifting the club around with your hands to find the right plane.

It's easy to see where the idea of holding a headcover under your lead arm started. After all, if you're trying to initiate the downswing with your body turn and create that pressure between your chest and the lead bicep, holding the headcover in there would reinforce that pressure, right?

Yes, but dialing up the pressure for the entire swing takes away that accelerating factor you need for good clubhead speed. You want to feel the chest turn and put pressure on your lead bicep, but you would want the headcover to fall out right after that pressure hits—as if you've just hit the accelerator. The arms use that pressure as a jumping off point to speed up and move in front of the chest, not drag behind.

If you were to hold that head cover under your arm the whole way through your swing, you're only going to be able to generate speed with your chest. Your lead arm will stay "stuck" to you chest and you'll feel like your swing has stalled.

# NOTES

# 6

## DON'T FLIP
## YOUR WRISTS

The longest hitters on the PGA Tour swing the driver with around 120 miles per hour of clubhead speed. The average amateur player swings around 90 miles per hour.

As different as those speeds are, the same thing is true for both of those swings. Impact happens literally in the blink of an eye—way too quickly to have any kind of precise control over what's going on.

But for years, players and teachers have been using photographs or paused frames from a video to examine what various swing positions look like frozen in time, and to try to get people to copy those static positions during what is supposed to be a dynamic, fluid motion.

Those stop action moments have caused more players more grief and struggle than just about anything else in the game.

Why?

Because a lot of the commentary and instruction that comes out of those frozen moments has to do with what the wrists and hands do—or should be doing—down through impact.

A still photograph of a really good player shows that he or she has a flat or slightly arched lead wrist at impact. The reflex response by teachers through the years has been to tell students that a flat lead wrist is the goal to hitting solid shots. So they try to get the student to eliminate wrist "action" in the swing to keep from "flipping" or "scooping" shots. Generations of players have actually been afraid to use their wrists at all, because they've always heard that any wrist movement or breakdown is bad.

The problem is, good players do have a flat or slightly arched lead wrist at impact, but wrist angles are impossible to detect with photographs.

In reality—and we have the technology to show it—a good player's wrists are going through a tremendous change in position, and in two different axes of movement. They're using their wrists a lot.

Hold your hands out in front of you as if you're about to clap your hands. Now bend your wrists so that the fingers on each hand are pointing toward the target. Your wrists are moving on a horizontal axis—notice how the left one is now bent (or extended) and the right is arched (or flexed). Now bend your wrists in the opposite direction, so that your fingers are pointed

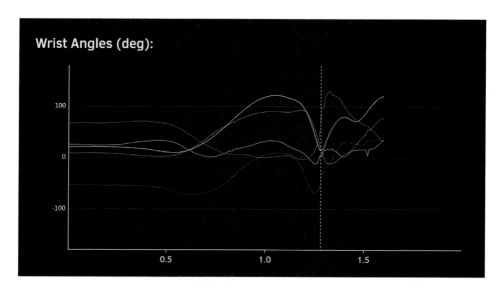

This graph—of Greg Norman's wrist
movements through the swing—shows
that the wrists are anything but quiet or
flat throughout. Good players use their
wrists to transfer energy to the golf club.

away from the target. Now your wrists are in the opposite con-
dition—the left one is arched (or flexed) and the right is bent (or
extended)

With your hands out in front of you in the clapping position
again, the wrist movement that hinges your hands upward and
downward is the second axis, called deviation, which is cocking
and uncocking in golf terminology.

Now that we have those terms down, it's easier to describe
what is really happening with a good player's wrists during a
swing, and what you should be doing instead of trying to freeze
yours.

It's almost a cliche at this point, but good wrist movement
starts with a good grip. If you hold the club the right way, with

the handle straight across the first joints of your fingers, you're giving your trailing wrist the freedom to move, and giving your lead wrist the ability to absorb a lot of active flexion from the trailing wrist without collapsing too early. By far the most common bad grip is one where the handle runs across the palm. When you hold the club this way, the motion of the swing will promote the wrong kind of wrist action, where the trailing wrist flexes and the lead wrist collapses toward the target too early.

Another problem that sabotages good wrist movement is bad body motion. For example, if you don't rotate your upper body on the downswing, the only way to actually hit the ball successfully is to throw your wrists at the ball.

It isn't crucial to understand every element of Greg Norman's wrist movements in this graph, but what it does is give you an overall view of how much the wrists are moving at any given point during the swing. As you can see, this is about as far away from keeping your wrists frozen or flat throughout the swing as possible. The good player's lead wrist is flat for a moment in time, but is moving toward extension right after impact. He or she is using the wrists and forearms for extra dynamic motion and power through the ball. It's taking full advantage of all the energy you've stored in the backswing and the first part of the downswing.

If you do actually try to create that artificial flat position with your lead wrist, you're creating some problems that will have to be overcome with compensations in your swing. Holding that flat or slightly arched position with the lead wrist through the last part of the downswing creates too much forward lean of the club. The excess forward lean pushes the low point of your swing too far forward and skews your path inside-out, and prevents

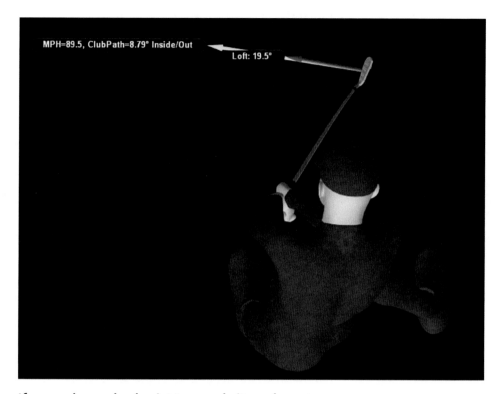

MPH=89.5, ClubPath=8.79° Inside/Out

Loft: 19.5°

**If you arch your lead wrist too much, it produces too much forward lean in the shaft and a swing path skewed to the right. You won't launch the ball at the ideal trajectory, and it will be hard to hold greens.**

you from flighting shots with the right trajectory.

Instead of trying to "control" the wrists and the clubhead down through impact, you're going to produce more speed and, ultimately, more control over your ball if you learn to let the momentum of the club help you move your wrists in a more dynamic way.

That doesn't mean you get to the top of your backswing and just forget about your wrists. You do have to activate them on purpose with some sense of timing. But that's something any player can develop by working on a simple drill using a table top.

Sit with a club in your hands and face a wooden table top that is the same height as your belly button. Set your arms in your normal address position and line up the chair so that the club-head is resting right up against the leading edge of the table.

When you set up, there's this natural amount of what's called offset angle—the angle between the club and the lead arm. If the club is directly in line with arm, there's no offset. When you grip the club low in the hand, where the fingers and palm meet, you have an offset angle of about 10-25 degrees. When you're set up to the table top like this, the natural offset angle of your wrists will put you in a position so that your hands are below the level of the table to start.

Now, if you make your normal backswing with your upper body, you'll see and feel your arms moving above the surface of the table. On the downswing, your goal is to produce arm and wrist movement that will return the clubhead to the leading edge of the table at impact—but with your hands below the level of the table top as they were when they started.

If you try to "create" lag by restricting the release of the club-head in the downswing, your hands will never drop below the level of the table top, and you not only won't square the club-head but you'll also be giving up a lot of speed.

Make some slower swings feeling your hands moving down under the level of the table during the downswing and then your wrist snapping the club into alignment onto the edge of the ta-ble. The flexion and extension of your wrists will let you "wipe" the clubhead right down along the leading edge of that table top through the area of what would be impact with a ball.

Now, there are different ways to return the clubhead to the

edge of the table with the hands below. Two different examples are a David Toms-style swing and a Rickie Fowler-type action. They're both perfectly legitimate ways to do it. David's arms would move down from very high above the table and return the clubhead to the edge of the table relatively early in the downswing. Rickie's arms would come in from a shallower angle, and he'd snap the clubhead onto the edge relatively late.

But both players are actively using their wrists to release the club in the downswing—not hold off or prevent wrist movement. They're both just doing it in productive ways.

In the tabletop drill, make a downswing motion with your arms and wrists so that you return the clubhead to the edge of the table with your hands below its surface.

# NOTES

# 7

## SWING DOWN THE LINE

**A**lmost every chapter in this book has at least mentioned the problem of "coming over the top," even if it's just briefly.

It's not because we don't have anything else to talk about.

It's because it's the dominant part of the most common swing pattern in the game. If you're hitting a mixture of weak, high shots to the right or pulled banana slices, you're probably coming over the top—or swinging the club out and across the target line early in the downswing and swiping across the ball.

Given that millions of players have had this problem over the years, it's not a big surprise that advice like "swing down the line" has become a fixture in golf instruction.

The thinking goes like this: If you're swinging from over the top, your path is coming from outside the target line and moving across to the left. By swinging "down the line," you're trying to move the clubhead toward the target for longer—presumably to keep it from crossing over to the left.

If you're a player who has struggled with coming over the top and tried that tip without seeing positive results, you won't be surprised to hear that it doesn't fix the real problem.

As we've been talking about in the Lag and Pause at the Top chapters, downswing problems like that happen because the body is moving out of sequence from the top of the backswing.

Trying to manually re-route your club with your arms won't fix those body sequence issues. And if you actually do try to swing "down the line," you're just adding another problem on top of the ones you already have. You're not really doing anything to change your swing. You're just changing where the club "exits"—or moves up into the follow-through after going through the hitting zone.

The crucial thing to remember here is that no matter what you do—swing over the top, try to swing down the line, any-thing—the club will release. There are no straight lines in golf. Artificially trying to push the club down the line—or in any other direction—is just going to disrupt what the club was built to do, which is swing on an arc.

Before anyone holds up Lee Trevino as the ultimate example of a player who really swung the club down the line—and was one of the great ball-strikers of all time—it's important to keep a few facts about Mr. Trevino in mind. He played with an extreme

Lee Trevino's stance, forward torso bend
and club position near the finish made it
look like he swung the club down the line,
but as you can see here, the club still exits
to the left of the target line after impact.

open stance and his body was extremely bent forward at impact, two factors that made it appear as though he was swinging "down the line" much more than he really was.

When you watch a great player—Trevino included—hit shots from the down-the-line perspective, where you're on the target line behind them and looking out toward the target, you see the same thing happen. After impact, the player's arms disappear, because the swing is moving around the body—not down the line. When the club reappears, the shaft comes up and bisects the shoulder. The arms move up and around into the finish as a result of the momentum of the downswing—not because of any effort to push them anywhere.

Ironically enough, all of this advice also applies to the player who is at the opposite end of the spectrum from the one with the over-the-top move. If you hook the ball because you swing on an extreme inside-to-out path—from close to the body out across the target line on the way through the ball—you've also

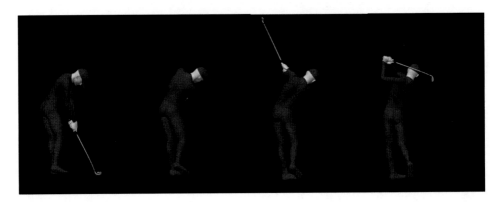

In a good follow-
through, the club
disappears after
impact from the
down-the-line view
and then the club
and hands exit in line
with the shoulders.

probably heard that swinging "down the line" instead of so far to
the right is going to help you.

But, just like the slicers, you need to improve your body
movement and transition instead of trying to artificially manip-
ulate the arc of your swing.

No matter if you're missing shots right or left, you can use the
same shadow drill in conjunction with the body movement tips
we talked about in the other chapters to check that the club is
exiting where it should.

Set up in your living room or basement so that a light source
is shining your shadow on the wall in front of you—as if you were
hitting an imaginary shot toward the wall.

Now, make some three-quarter swings paying close attention
to where the shaft of the club crosses your shoulder in both the

backswing and the follow-through. When the arms are parallel to the ground on the backswing and follow-through, the shadow of the shaft should appear to be coming directly out of your shoulder. Training your swing shape this way will help you gain more control over your ball flight and hit more fairways and greens.

# NOTES

# 8

# KEEP YOUR HEAD DOWN

I f you built a spreadsheet that counted the number of times each nugget of swing advice has been passed around over the last 120 years, some variation of "keep your head down" or "keep your head still" would rank right up near the top.

Whether it's Jack Grout holding onto the hair at the front of Jack Nicklaus' head or a 90-shooter trying to help a friend at the driving range, the whole "head down" idea has been a go-to piece of advice for decades.

It's easy to see where it came from. Long before we had 3D motion capture, video (or even photography), teachers relied on what they saw, and what the ball did. The idea that you need to really focus your vision on the ball—and keep your head locked in position to do that—made intuitive sense.

And for at least the last 100 years, players who have lots of extra head movement toward or away from the ball or side to side have really struggled to hit the ball consistently in the middle of the face. When you're struggling with mishit after mishit, hitting grounders or taking big chunks of turf, you're definitely a target for some well-meaning advice.

But the problem with a generic comment like "keep your head still" or "keep your eye on the ball" is that it doesn't address the specific problems you (or any other player) might have. Worse yet, if you actually are able to follow the advice and keep your head locked down and "still," you might feel more quiet over the ball through impact, but you're also blocking yourself from ever having any dynamic motion and speed in your swing.

Let's start with the first piece. Lots of head movement toward or away from the ball is a symptom of serious issues in your golf swing.

For example, if your head abruptly moves away from the ball in the downswing, it means you're out-of-sequence in your swing. It's your brain's instinctive response—backing your torso away from the ground to give the club room to actually get to the ball without smashing into the turf a foot behind the ball.

If you try to push your head down to stop from "looking up," you're going to force that club to hit the ground too early, or force your body to pull up while your head stays down. It only takes a couple of times crashing the club into the ground a foot behind the ball before you reflexively start backing your body up to get room to hit the ball. The rebound action of your head responding to the body backing up is the "you lifted your head" moment your playing partner sees when he or she is trying to give some well-meaning (but inaccurate) advice.

When the head moves a bunch from side to side, it is usually a symptom instead of an issue by itself. The head and torso usually move laterally in response to the interaction between the upper and lower body. If you make a backswing and excessively straighten your back leg, your head is going to move in response. It's going to topple forward. If you push too aggressively toward the target on the downswing, you're going to disturb the turn of your body and your head will wobble.

If you respond to any of those issues by working on locking your head in place, all you're going to do is limit how much your torso can turn. When your torso can't turn, you're producing all of your power and speed in the swing with your arms. You're going to hit shorter shots, and you won't be any more consistent. It will feel like you're out of balance, and that your arms are out of control because they're doing so much without the body participating. Without enough torso rotation through impact, you're

going to see and feel your lead elbow bend into the classic "chicken wing" position.

And, ironically, you'll be "moving" your head even more than you were before because you'll

**Locking your head in position forces your left arm away from the body through impact into the classic chicken wing position.**

be doing so much with the muscles in your neck to counter-act the motion of the rest of your body. Through the shot, your brain will also be subconsciously reminding you that you've lost all that speed from your body turn going away, so you move your head and shoulders even more in a desperate, late lurch.

So what's the answer?

Instead of worrying so much about anchoring your head, the goal should be to feel it moving in response to the body in a stable way. Picture the center point between your shoulders as being stable, while giving your head and neck freedom to move.

Instead of initiating your takeback with your shoulders or arms, feel like you're first pushing an accelerator pedal with your left foot. Your torso will respond, and your head will accommo-date that movement.

On the downswing, you're going to initiate with your feet again (as we talked about in Chapter 3), pushing and twisting with your trail foot and feeling the force on your lead foot push back behind you to assist the left hip in rotating open.

It's important to remember that in an ideal swing, your hips and left shoulder are going to be moving up through impact. You want your head to respond to this movement, which means it's naturally going to rise slightly (not abruptly). Forcing your head down is just going to prevent your arms and club from swinging through with speed and precision.

Precisely defining "ideal" head movement is hard because it's so dependent on how each person swings the club. But in gen-eral terms, the good players move their heads in different ways, but they keep their upper torso pretty stable.

Take Rickie Fowler and Greg Norman as examples. They're both world-class players, and they both have dramatically

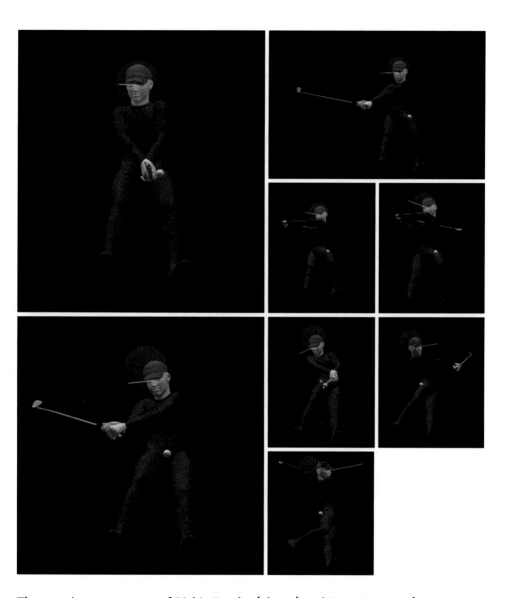

These swing sequences of Rickie Fowler (above) and Greg Norman (next page) show just how much the head really moves during the swing—and how differently it can move between two world-class players. The yellow halo indicates the head position at address, and the yellow line shows how much the head is turning in relation to the body during every part of the swing.

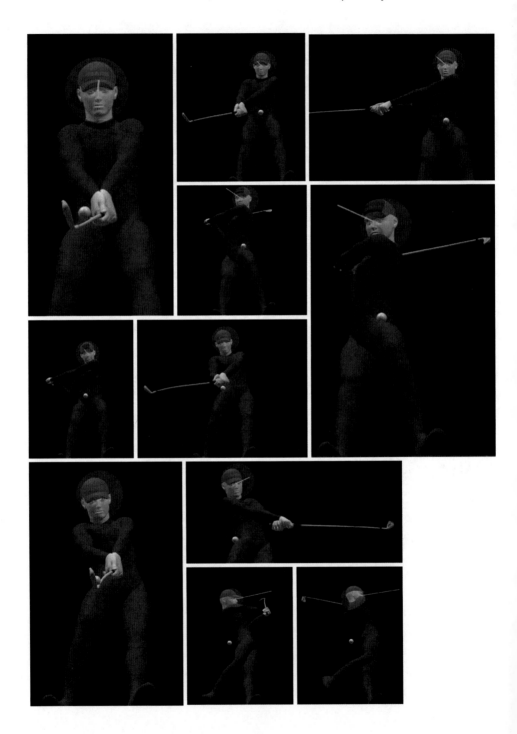

different head movement through the swing. Both before and after his work with Butch Harmon, Fowler has a downswing you can identify from all the way across the golf course. His head stays turned toward the ball longer during the downswing, but it still moves around ahead and above his right shoulder coming through impact. Greg Norman's head flows into almost the same position as Fowler's in the backswing, but he lets it turn toward the target earlier in his downswing.

A great way to reinforce the feeling of a stable torso with head and neck freedom is to find your favorite swiveling office chair. Sit in it and hold a golf club up in front of you, so your hands are centered in the middle of your chest. Using your feet to push on the ground, swivel your body in the chair in your backswing direction. Keep facing forward and your head centered over your torso as you do it, but don't lock anything in place. When you get to the end of the turn in the chair, you'll feel your head turn a little in response to the shoulders getting to the end of their journey. Start your downswing by pushing with your feet, then turn your torso through in your downswing direction, and again let your head stay centered over your torso and respond to your shoulders when they get near the end of their turn.

It's this mix of a stable upper torso and dynamic body movement that lets Tour players produce tremendous speed, but with precision and control. Nothing is locked down, but they don't have out-of-control head and upper torso movement back and forth or up and down.

X Golf School - Players with a 2 Handicap and Better - Average of Head Movements

| MOTION | Address Position | Half Backswing | Top of Backswing | Impact | Half Follow Thru | Finish |
|---|---|---|---|---|---|---|
| HEAD TURNING | Zero | 6 degrees closed | 14 degrees closed | 5 degrees open | 16 degrees open | 86 degrees open |
| HEAD LIFTING AND DROPPING | Zero | .2 inches down | .1 inches down | 2.8 inches down | 2.2 inches down | 9 inches up |
| HEAD SIDE TO SIDE SWAY | Zero | 1.8 inches right | 2 inches right | 2 inches left | 3.2 inches left | 11.8 inches left |
| HEAD THRUST FORWARD/ BACKWARD | Zero | .1 inches back | .7 inches forward | 1 inch back | 1.8 inches back | 7.6 inches back |

**We've collected data for years on how the head moves during the swing. Here's a summary of those results.**

# NOTES

# 9

## TIPS OF
## THE FUTURE

**W**e've spent a lot of time talking about some of the ways instruction tips have knocked players sideways over the last 20 years. We're going to finish the book by looking forward instead of backward, to introduce two ideas we think will be at the forefront of golf instruction for the next 20 years.

The first idea is centered on impact, and what you can learn from something that's happening so fast that even some of the best cameras in the world can't capture it.

The second idea focuses on the path the right elbow takes

during the swing, and what it can tell you about your potential as a player.

## IMPACT

Impact is what keeps you coming back day after day to this great game, so let's start with that.

It's the moment of truth, literally and figuratively. All the things you're doing in your swing with your body and club are designed to get to impact with speed and precision. The ball actually spends 4/10,000ths of a second on the clubface—so fast that by the time you're registering the vibrations and can react to them, the ball is already at least 10 yards on its way.

Impact happens so fast that it's impossible to consciously control what's happening to the club within the moment, but you can get some great clues about what to work on in your game with some basic examination and perception.

Let's talk about the literal "feel" of impact. Even if you're a relative beginner, you know the difference between a really well struck ball in the center of the face and a mishit that clanks off the heel or the toe.

Nobody likes hitting shots that miss the center of the face, but the damage they cause is greater than just the loss of yardage or crookedness of the flight. If you're consistently mishitting shots, it seriously affects your grip. Because you're subconsciously aware that you need to stabilize the club to handle the unpleasant vibrations caused by a mishit, you squeeze the grip tighter.

When you squeeze the grip tighter, you promote all different kinds of problems along the sequence. It's harder for tight arms and shoulders to make a full backswing. When your hands and forearms are tight, it's harder to release the club in a natural way with good speed.

In other words, the act of bracing yourself for mishits actually produces more mishits. If you're struggling with producing solid impact and experiencing a lot of tension, it may be time to scale back a bit and start to work on the basic shape of your swing. Start with a few hitting sessions where you only work on small shots—since the slower speed of small swings will give you more time and control over the shape of your swing path and the trajectory of the clubhead. Mix in the tabletop and shadow drills we talked about in the earlier chapters, which will also give you nuts-and-bolts training in how the club should be moving.

Just like the feel in your hands, the divot you leave—or don't leave—also tells a story.

Admit it. You've watched tour players hit a full pitching wedge approach shot and have been fascinated by the huge strip of turf they sometimes flop into the air.

You've probably even gone out and tried to get more "aggressive" with your own wedges and hit down on it more to produce a more downward strike and increased backspin.

How did that work out for you?

In reality, you don't need to be worrying about actually trying to make a divot. The best divots are light scrapes of turf with the short irons, and almost no scrape at all with the middle and long irons.

What really produces a divot is the ball position you chose for the shot and the playing characteristics of the club in your hand. The more loft a club has, the more it gets pushed into the ground when it hits the ball. And the faster the club is moving, the more turf gets taken.

When the club is waist high on the downswing, as shown here with Rickie Fowler's avatar, the hands have already reached their low point. From here, they'll move upward through impact.

When you're watching a tour player produce that big divot, it's happening because he's swinging a super high lofted club with a lot of speed—not because he's smashing down on the ball as hard as he can.

Here's the big idea you need to take away about divots. On a properly struck shot, your hands have already reached the lowest point on their journey by the time they've reached your trail thigh. From there they're moving upward and inward while the club is whipping to its own lowest point in the impact area. If you're trying to intentionally hit down on the ball by moving your hands downward through impact, you're costing yourself a huge amount of speed—and you aren't even generating more spin.

Pictured above, Rickie Fowler is at the stage of the swing where his hands have reached their low point.

This final phase of the downswing consists of a very small

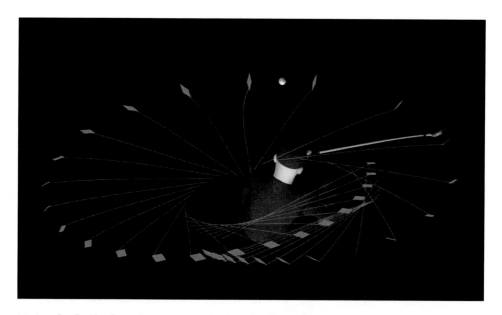

**Not only do the hands move up during the last phase of the downswing—they also move in, toward the body. In Fowler's swing, shown here, it helps him whip the club through the ball with a lot of speed.**

amount of hand travel and a large amount of club whip into the ball.

For great ball strikers, hand low point is the closest the grip of the club will ever get to the target line on the downswing. From that point on, the hands of the golfer move up and in. It should feel as though the grip of the club is going to harpoon the inside of your left thigh as the head of the club races towards the ball. If you're struggling with inconsistent contact, you're probably working under the idea that you should be driving your hands down toward the ball all the way to impact. This "hit down" advice has created a generation of golfers who apply too much force "across the club" and not enough force "towards the golfer"—which is what produces maximum club head speed.

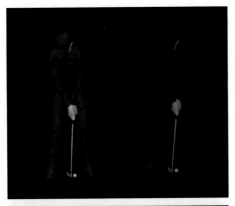

**The differences in right elbow position between Rickie Fowler in gold and a 6-handicapper in blue are dramatic.**

A great way to feel your hands move correctly is to swing down to thigh high in the downswing, but execute the final phase while letting your right hand slide down the club toward the head as you move towards impact. The end result will be a hockey-style split grip, but more importantly, you're creating the right movements with the handle end of the club. It promotes the sensation that the two hands on the grip are cancelling each other out. One hand isn't doing anything to dominate the other.

**THE MAGIC RIGHT ELBOW**

TrackMan fanatics love to point to radar data to "prove" a player is an elite ballstriker. But you don't need to see that somebody has "zeroed out" his TrackMan measurements to know that he or she is getting the most out of the swing.

One of the biggest differ-

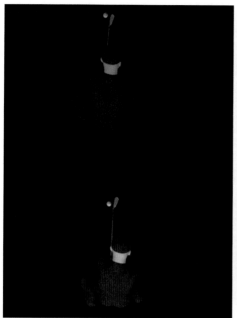

**If you visualize the location of the tag on Fowler's shirt, in gold, it actually moves toward the target during the backswing, while the 6-handicapper's shifts away.**

ences between tour-level players and even single-digit handicappers is what happens to the right elbow through the course of the swing. It might be the one body part that behaves the most differently between the two kinds of golfers—and it's something you can fix in a pretty straightforward way.

Let's compare Rickie Fowler (*gold avatar*) to a 6-handicap player Mike has measured in his Long Island studio. We'll call the amateur player Rod (*blue avatar*).

At address, Rickie's arms are nice and relaxed, and his right elbow has 20 degrees of bend. Rod's arms are also relaxed, but his

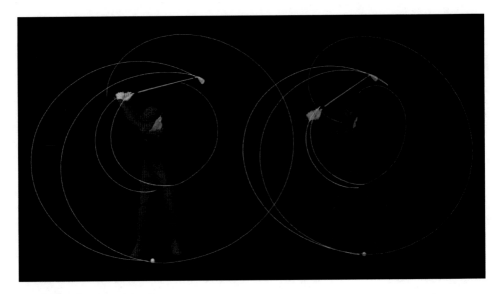

**Fowler's hands move down
on a narrow path, while the
6-handicapper's come down
on pretty much the same path
as they went up.**

right elbow is 6 degrees bent. As they move into their backswings, the difference really starts to show itself.

Halfway back, Rickie's right elbow is bent slightly more than at the start, 30 degrees, while Rod's has increased to 90 degrees.

Top of Backswing, you can clearly see the differences in the right elbow as Rickie is just shy of 85 degrees and Rod is in excess of 90 degrees.

They've basically moved their right elbows in completely opposite ways.

Now, your first reaction to this information is probably to say to yourself, "Ok, I need to extend my arm more on the backswing." Doing that without changing anything else will just cause your swing more harm than good.

The real reason the two players have such different right elbow positions is because of how they turn their bodies in the backswing. It's here where you can make a change that will produce extremely positive results.

Looking at GEARS images from behind and above, we can focus on a point that's basically where the tag on a player's shirt would be—which serves as a center point for the upper body.

When Fowler makes his backswing, the tag on his shirt remains stabilized and actually moves slightly toward the target as his shoulders turn. He's created plenty of room in his backswing for his extended right arm to move down on a narrower path.

Compare that to what happens to the tag on Rod's shirt. He starts his backswing with an upper body push away from the ball and not stable rotation. Because he's moved behind the ball, he doesn't have room to keep the right elbow extended, and has to throw the clubhead earlier in the downswing.

It doesn't mean Rod can't hit decent shots. He does. But he isn't as consistent or powerful as the guy who finished in the top five in all four majors in 2014.

# NOTES

You go into a project like this with a vision of what you want it to look like at the end. Thanks to Matthew Rudy and Tim Oliver, it surpasses anything we could have imagined. The technical side of golf instruction can be challenging to read and understand, but Matt helped us make a book that is true to the science but easy for any player to understand and use. The package Tim put it in with his design is amazing as well. We can't wait to do it again.